The Conflict Resolution Library™

Dealing with Secrets

• Don Middleton •

The Rosen Publishing Group's
PowerKids Press™
New York

This book is dedicated to my wife, Sue; my daughters, Jody and Kim; my mother-in-law, Mim; and my parents, Bernice and Helmut Bischoff. Also, special thanks to authors and friends Diana Star Helmer and Tom Owens for believing in me. —Don Middleton

Published in 1999 by The Rosen Publishing Group, Inc.
29 East 21st Street, New York, NY 10010

Photo Credits and Photo Illustrations: p. 4 © Jim Cummins/FPG International; p. 7 © Michael Goldman/FPG International; pp. 8, 19 by Seth Dinnerman; pp. 11, 16 by Carrie Grippo; p. 12 © Dusty Willison/International Stock; p. 15 by Matt Harnett; p. 20 by Ira Fox.

First Edition

Layout and design: Erin McKenna

Middleton, Don.
    Dealing with secrets / Don Middleton.
            p.   cm. — (The conflict resolution library)
    Includes index.
Summary: Describes secrets, why people have them, when and with whom to share them, and the
        difference between good and bad secrets.
    ISBN 0-8239-5265-7
    1. Children's secrets—Juvenile literature. [1. Secrets.] I. Title. II. Series.
    HQ784.S42M53 1998
    155.4'18—dc21   98-22631
                                                                              CIP
                                                                               AC

Manufactured in the United States of America

Contents

What Is a Secret?

A secret is a thought that you want to keep to yourself. Or a secret might be something someone else asked you not to tell anyone. A friend may have told you that he or she did poorly on a test, but the friend might not want you to tell other people. Other secrets may be your **private** (PRY-vit) feelings. It's okay to have secrets.

◀ Friends often share secrets.

Sharing Secrets

Sometimes you may need to share your secret with another person. Sharing a secret can make the secret less scary or more exciting. It depends on what your secret is.

If your secret is making you feel bad, it might help to tell the secret to someone you **trust** (TRUHST). You may be able to get some helpful **advice** (ad-VYS). Parents are usually good people to share secrets with. Or you may want to share your secret with a close friend.

Sharing a secret can be easier than dealing with a problem by yourself. ▶

The Surprise Birthday Party

The surprise birthday party for Kim is tonight. All the kids are talking about it. Then Kim walks into the classroom. Suddenly everyone is silent.

"Hi! What are you guys doing?" Kim asks.
"Nothing. We were just talking," Jody says.

Later that night, at the party, Kim asks her best friend, "Jody, is this what you were all talking about this morning?"
"Yes! But I didn't want to tell you the secret and spoil the surprise," Jody answers.

◀ Some secrets are fun to keep!

Keeping Others' Secrets

At one time or another, each of us has been asked to keep a secret. Maybe you knew what your parents bought your brother for his birthday. Or your best friend told you that his parents are not living together anymore.

When you know a secret, it can be hard not to tell someone else. But remember that your friend is counting on you to keep his secret. When we are able to keep secrets, people learn to trust us.

People will tell you their secrets if ▶
they know they can trust you.

False Secrets That Hurt

Sometimes people make up things about others that aren't true. These false secrets can be lies or **rumors** (ROO-murz) that hurt someone else.

A rumor may be started by accident. A rumor may spread that a kid was caught cheating on a test, or that a classmate stole things. Before you know it, people begin to believe these stories. This hurts the **innocent** (IN-uh-sent) person.

◀ Be careful not to spread rumors.

13

The Stolen Magazines

After class, John and his friends often stop at a comic-book store. One day John was called to the principal's office.

"John, do you know anything about stolen comic books?" the principal asked.

"I don't like to tattle," said John.

"Telling the truth when someone steals isn't tattling," Mr. Lisowski said.

"Well . . . I saw Tim hide two books in his coat."

John was glad he no longer had to keep that secret.

Sometimes you need to share a secret with an adult. ▶

Scary Secrets

Some things must not be kept secret. Your best friend may tell you that something bad happened while a baby-sitter was looking after her. She may ask you to keep it a secret. Neither of you should keep bad things a secret. Together, you and your friend should tell a trusted adult. If someone touches you in a way you don't like, or says things that scare you, tell a grown-up you trust. Never keep it a secret, no matter what the person told you to do.

◀ Grown-ups will be able to help you with a scary secret.

Joanne and Marcia

"What's wrong?" Joanne asked her friend.
"Nothing! Just go away," Marcia shouted.
"Please tell me what's wrong," Joanne said.
"My baby-sitter hurt me," Marcia whispered.
"What do you mean?" asked Joanne.
"She hit me. My lip got cut." Marcia cried.
"We need to tell your mom," Joanne said.
"The baby-sitter said to keep it a secret,"
Marcia said.
"That's a bad secret. Let's go tell your mom,"
Joanne said. Marcia began to feel better.

A friend can help you share a scary ▶
secret with your parents.

Knowing Whom to Trust

We all decide whom we can trust with our secrets. Maybe you have an older brother or sister or a friend whom you trust. Sharing your feelings and secrets with people you trust can make problems easier to solve.

You must be careful not to share your secrets with people you don't know very well or don't trust. Take the time to get to know your friends. It takes time to build trust.

◀ It's better to share secrets with someone you've known for a long time.

Secrets Between Friends

Trust is a big part of friendship. When a friend tells you something in **confidence** (KON-fih-dens), you keep it a secret. But if the secret is about something bad, or wrong, or hurtful, you and your friend should not keep this secret. You can ask a trusted adult for help.

Try to help your friends with scary secrets. But remember you can have fun, silly secrets too!

Glossary

advice (ad-VYS) An opinion about how to handle a situation.

confidence (KON-fih-dens) A secret.

innocent (IN-uh-sent) Not guilty.

private (PRY-vit) Something that you keep to yourself.

rumor (ROO-mur) An opinion that is heard by a lot of people with no proof that it's true.

trust (TRUHST) To be able to rely on someone.

Index